Get Well Soon !

Activity & Puzzle Book
for Women

Crosswords, Word Finds,
Sudoku, Mandalas to Color,
Inspirational Quotes, Fun Quizzes,
Jokes and Trivia

Wishing this book provides you a little fun and distraction and that you're feeling better soon!

CROSSWORD 1

Across

1 Tumbler
6 Direct
10 Not straight
11 Switch words (2-3)
12 Link
13 Jinx
15 Tree trauma (4,3)
18 "Vamoose!" (3-3)
21 Twisted
22 See circled squares
24 Military specialist (5,5)
25 An American in Paris, maybe
26 Checks

Down

1 Kind of tax
2 Alternately (2,3,3)
3 Record holder
4 Short distance (6,5)
5 Green perimeters
7 Fairy tale character
8 "Of course" (7,8)
9 Kind of doll
14 Cherish (4,4)
16 Like some pitches
17 Out
19 Title bandit in a Verdi opera
20 Out of control (2,1,4)
22 Kind of board
23 Silents star Bara

Acid Rain
All Natural
Bamboo
Carbon Neutral
Clean Air Act
Compost
Earth Day
Earth-friendly
Ecosystem
El Nino
Endangered
Extinct
Fertility
Flood
Forest
Mass Transit
Organic
Ozone Layer
Pesticide
Population
Radioactive
Recycle
Recycling
Sand Storm
Sewage
Smog
Sustainable
Tsunami

```
O Z O N E L A Y E R T I K J Y F M E W
S A N D S T O R M S T X V S O L Z Q E
V U D S X L Z E O K H I E Z M O N F A
C G S L R G L P X X A V S E G O Q E T
T L Q T W E M O B T I V T V Q D G M H
F G E Q A O C N I T I S Y E S A F A E
E P M A C I I Y C L N L G W P O C R R
R B N P N M N A C S J A C E P E R I C
T O W W A A O A O L R L S T O S E D Z
I J R N I I I C B T I L B A P T S R E
L E U G D N E R U L S N R R U I T A N
I S L A A N D E A C E A G I L C D I D
T M R N R N N F G C A T D A A I F N A
Y A W Q I N I O A C T U A N T D G C N
B X L A O N X C U R D R N C I E M H G
B A M B O O O V F M M A N P O D F W E
E A R T H F R I E N D L Y Z N B S N R
M A S S T R A N S I T V R E C Y C L E
C G V M N D K F E A R T H D A Y T P D
```

SUDOKU 1 - EASY

7	4							
					1			
		2			9		4	8
	5				4			
					7	5	2	
2		3						1
1			9			8		
		6		8		7	9	
	2				3		5	

							■					■
								■				■
											,	
				■		■			■			
						■						
	■					.	■					
N	O	O	T	I	A	Y	G	E	V	E	R	Y
	I	T	O	H	L	I	I	D	I	E		
	P	B	P	D	I	S		B	O	Y		
	N	M	U	T	N	G		S	L	S		
	E	H	O	S	E			A				
			P		N							

imponderables...

Why isn't phonetic spelled the way it sounds??

Puzzle 2

■	■					■			■				■	■
■	■						■							
					■				■			■		
				■				■			■			
■			■						■				▨ .	■
H	Y	N	P	E	Y	E	A	I	S	C	T	N	A	I	T	O	D
N	A	O	U	I	N	S	E	N	T		T	E	T	T	H	N	W
	I	P	P	T	R	E	P	T	T		E	O	N	A			
		L	E	R	C	E	R		Y	H	U						
		E		F		C	O		W	O							

Puzzle 3

		■			■						■			
						■								■
■						■			■					
				■			■				■			
■	■	■	■						▨ .	■	■	■	■	■
I	A	T	K	E	T	T	O	R	O	M	E	S	T	U	R
F	O	R	I	A	L	D	G	H	I	M	E	N	T	S	E
D	T	C	U	S	S	I	U	M	S	E	U		T	H	
			H	S		T	W	E	T	N	G		O		

HOW COMPETITIVE ARE YOU?

Do you have a healthy approach to competition? Take this quiz to find out! (and if you feel the need to look at the answers...add 2 points to your final score)!

Some people think that I'm too competitive	true		false	
It takes a killer instinct to get ahead	true		false	
I have let someone else win	true		false	
I enjoy testing my skills against others	true		false	
I am at my best when competing with others	true		false	
I often try to beat the car next to me after a red light	true		false	
I turn almost everything into a contest	true		false	
I will be upset if I don't do well on this quiz	true		false	
I use a to-do list almost every day	true		false	
I have well defined goals	true		false	
I feel the need to be better than my siblings	true		false	
I am constantly learning new things	true		false	
I am a workaholic	true		false	
Score 1 point for each true answer. TOTAL =				

WHAT DOES YOUR SCORE MEAN?

0-4...You're actually anti-competitive. You are avoiding competitive situations which might mean you need a little more self-confidence. Some competition is a powerful motivator that helps you get ahead and contribute more.

5-8...You have a healthy level of competition. Keep up the good work!

9-13...You're going to be mad, but sorry, you didn't win this quiz! There's no denying your competitive nature and desire to succeed is a commendable quality, but stopping at nothing to come out on top can also become a problem when your competitiveness becomes all-consuming or takes the enjoyment away from others. Try to relax a little more!

You are
loued !

CROSSWORD 2

Across

2 Contract negotiator: Abbr.
3 The Trojans of the N.C.A.A.
5 Gut reaction?
9 Guarded
10 "It doesn't matter"
12 "For shame!"
14 "Concentration" pronoun
15 "Uh-uh!" (3,4,2,6)
20 Hooters (4,4)
21 Most recent
22 "To ___ is human ..."
23 "No way!" (3,1,6)
24 Not your
25 "Help!"
27 Narc's org.
29 Steady
32 ___-Magnon
33 Officer's query to a speeder (6,3,4)
37 Final: Abbr.
38 Funny business
42 By and by
45 Do some roadwork
46 Maxima maker
47 Actress Winger

(numbers at the end of clues indicate multiple word answer and their letter count)

Down

1 Elated (7,4)
2 "Aladdin" monkey
3 "Yoo-hoo!" (2,4)
4 Loc. ___
6 "Feels Like the First Time" band
7 Lots (5,1,3)
8 Fast one (5,5)
11 Book before Daniel: Abbr.
13 Meteorological phenomenon (6,9)
16 Releases
17 Bartender? (4,5)
18 Burlap fiber
19 Meeting place
26 "Beat it!"
27 "How obvious!"
28 Balloon filler
30 Substantial
31 Whimper
33 "Do ___ Diddy Diddy" (1964 hit)
34 Dusk, to Donne
35 Seat of White Pine County, Nev.
36 Computer file suffix
39 "___ in Calico" (1946 song)
40 Hate group
41 "Ol' Man River" composer
43 Felt bad about
44 "___ lost!"

14

WORD FIND 2

Action
Awaken
Awareness
Balance
Being
Blessings
Breath
Celebrate
Choose
Clarity
Commit
Connect
Courage
Creativity
Design
Dream
Emotions
Engage
Experience
Family
Focus
Friends
Gifts
Gratitude
Happiness
Journey
JoyLightness
Living
Love
Nature
Nurture
Oneness
Possibility

Power
Prayer
Relaxation
Self
Share
Smile
Soul
Truth
Values
Wisdom

```
D T K E C F L I G H T N E S S S A G G
E C U X R O N E N O I T A X A L E R L
S E C P B C M E K S S E N E R A W A B
I N Y E V U N M K E T V N E J J U O L
G N J R L S V O I A R F Y C H O O S E
N O Q I T E A U W T W A I I E V K D S
Y C G E E C B I D N R A H G R A Q V S
X H K N P C S R J P R Q F S U L A S I
J Y Y C I D N M A S J I L B T U S B N
O T T E O V O A I T U O E Q U E O C G
U I I M L Y I E L L E M S Z N S O N S
R R V Y Y N T L G A E X E I J U I N J
N A I Y V M O J E A B Y P D R E A M P
E L T X F A M I L Y G P S A B T D C N
Y C A P O W E R H T A N G I U V M H O
Q D E B R E A T H H L E E R L O V E I
U F R B N R U H S S E N E N O U Y F T
B B C X Q R X Y T I L I B I S S O P C
P G R A T I T U D E F R I E N D S S A
```

	9		7		4	1	6	
	3			1	2			
1					6		9	3
3		7	8					6
				4				9
				6	5		1	
			6	2	9	7	5	8
5	8	9				6		4
	2							1

	5						2	
9			1			6		
6			2	8	3			
2		5	3					
7		6		1	2			
			7	4			9	
5		7	9	6		8		3
						1		6
1	6		4		7	2		

FALLEN QUOTES 4, 5

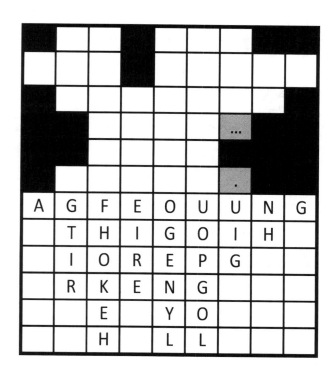

	S	S	Y	K	A	T	D	V	O	N	T	T	U	Y
		I	S	O	L	D	I	O	I	T	S	O	R	
		H	F	U	C	D	E	F	I	R	Y	T		
			U	C	U	E		D	N		G			
			O		Y			N						

Random Thoughts...

When everything is coming your way, you're in the wrong lane.

HOW DYSFUNCTIONAL IS YOUR FAMILY?

We all have that embarrassing uncle or some odd habits. See how your unique family compares to others!

Have you ever not spoken to another family member for months at a time?	yes		no	
Have you ever hung up on a family member?	yes		no	
Is there a family member that you dread inviting to events?	yes		no	
Does your family tree intersect ?	yes		no	
Has anyone in your family appeared on a daytime talk show?	yes		no	
Has anyone in your family gotten a restraining order against another family member?	yes		no	
Has someone in your family embarrassed you?	yes		no	
Is there regular yelling in your household?	yes		no	
When you compare family craziness with friends do you usually win?	yes		no	
Has anyone in your family run away from home?	yes		no	
Does your family gossip about each other?	yes		no	
Is your family very large or very small?	yes		no	
Score 1 point for each yes answer. TOTAL =				

WHAT DOES YOUR SCORE MEAN?

0-4 Seriously, your family is a little boring. But perfectly healthy and balanced. You should seriously consider marrying someone with a little more dysfunction just to keep things interesting.

5-8 Congratulations! Like most families yours is a little quirky and dysfunctional. Life would be a lttle boring otherwise.

9-16 Wow...your family is seriously dysfunctional. I hope someone will make some money on that book.

24

The obstacle

is the path

PRESIDENTIAL TRIVIA CROSSWORD 3

Across

3 Had a dog named Veto

5 Refused to use the telephone

8 Loved jelly beans

10 Was a fashion model

11 First president born in a log cabin

12 Acquired California during his term

13 Held the first Inaugural Ball

15 Only president born in California

18 In charge of D-Day invasion

19 Gave the White House its name

20 1st to name an African American to his cabinet

21 Succeeded Garfield upon his assassination

22 First President to be a Rhodes Scholar

Down

1 The only president from Indiana

2 Was a successful tailer

4 Once captured by pirates

6 First President spelunker

7 First President to wear pants

9 First to put a Christmas tree in the White House

11 Attended séances at the White House

12 The only bachelor President

14 On the $50

16 Great-great-great nephew of John Tyler

17 Had 15 children

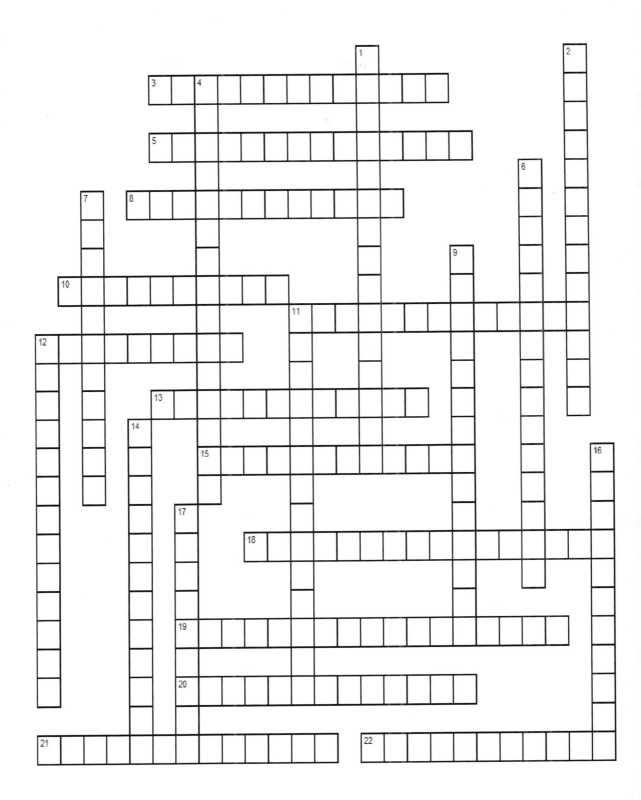

Adriatic
Aral Sea
Atlantic
Baikal
Baltic
Bass Sea
Black Sea
Caribbean
Chukotsk Sea
Cook Strait
Coral Sea
East China Sea
Flores Sea
Gulf of Oman
Hudson Bay
Irish Sea
Kara Sea
Lake Chad
Lake Erie
Lake Maracaibo
Loch Ness
North Sea
Pacific
Red Sea
Skaggerak
South China Sea
Strait of Malacca
Timor Sea
White Sea
Yellow Sea

```
C H U K O T S K S E A L P C G Z E
S A E M A T C Z K E B A I K A L J
T E N O E I J O S G C T D J H N B
R S Y L S M G D R I N S B A P A R
A E X O S O E U F A D T D C L E A
I T V B E R U I L L A Q T K B E I
T I C I R S C T A F E S I Q A B S
O H I A O E A K H S O C E X R I H
F W T C L A E Z S C C F I A E R T
M A A A F C S S E N H C O L G A R
A H I R H L A K E E R I E M G C O
L L R A T B K H U D S O N B A Y N
A V D M A E S L A R A V M A K N K
C K A E I A E S A N I H C T S A E
C O O K S T R A I T I S T R G E P
A B L A C K S E A I R I S H S E A
Y E L L O W S E A H K A R A S E A
```

	8		9			5	7	
2						1		
				3	4			
		3				2	9	
						4		
	9	2	7	6				
	1		4					9
						7		
			2	7	3		8	

		4			2			6
				1				7
6		1	7	3				
			6					
7				2	8			
	8			7			9	3
	2			5				8
5			1	8	9		7	

The grid and letter bank for the fallen quotes puzzle:

I	W	O	N	I	O	L	O	E	E	A	L	E	Y	P	E	T	O	D	I	M	I	R	E	E
F	O	R	R	T	R	F	N	O	V	A	D	N	K	L	Y	E	O	N		A	T	H
H		Y	O	U	H	T	M	E	L	I	L	I	E	U	R	Y	O	N		A	T
		L		A		S	E		N	O		M	O	S		O	U
		G		R				N

Random Thoughts...

If your dog is fat, you aren't getting enough exercise.

First grid letters:

```
F  A  T  H  T  T  O  N  P  T  D  R  E  A  D  C  A  M  P  T
N  O  M  L  T  T  I  A  G  D  T  O  S  A  H  T  R  N  D
S  O  I  A  I  H  E  U  L  N  G  T  A  U  C  O  E  E  D
         I     W  H  M  N           R  O  T  T  E  E
         E     N  G     A                    T
```

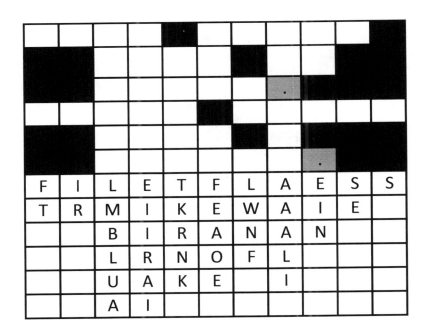

Second grid letters:

```
F  I  L  E  T  F  L  A  E  S  S
T  R  M  I  K  E  W  A  I  E
      B  I  R  A  N  A  N
      L  R  N  O  F  L
      U  A  K  E  I
      A  I
```

Life is

Beautiful

CROSSWORD 4

Across

3 "Scream" director Craven
6 Italian, e.g.
8 Rattles
11 Control
12 Discounted (2,4)
15 Be itinerant
16 Blah-blah-blah
17 His "4" was retired
18 "Thank You (Falettinme Be Mice ___ Again)" (#1 hit of 1970)
19 "And ___ bed"
21 Catch, in a way
23 Place to find keys (10,5)
25 Often memorized math term
27 Outer: Prefix
29 End of the question
30 Foolish
32 X's
33 "Keystone Kops" producer
34 Dear
35 Carve in stone
36 "___ the fields we go"
37 Phrase on the back of a buck (2,3,2,5)
38 Buttonwood
41 "Yes ___?" (2,2)
42 "That was a close one!"
43 Bout stopper, for short
44 "Duino Elegies" poet
45 Anemic (5-7)

Down

1 "Bravo!" (4,3)
2 End of the quote (5,6)
3 Ring org.
4 "Enough already!"
5 Response to "grazie"
6 Check mate?
7 No matter what (4,4,2,5)
9 Hack
10 Pan-fries
13 Cover letters?
14 Go ballistic (4,4,4)
20 Buckle (5,2,3,5)
22 "... ___ quit!"
24 Fails (4,2,3)
25 Dazed and confused
26 Head honcho (3,6)
28 Eager (5-6)
31 Prefix with -phile
35 Recluse
39 Sagan of "Cosmos"
40 Density symbol
42 Loan figure: Abbr.

(numbers at the end of clues indicate multiple word answer and their letter count)

Al Gore
Ann Rice
B. B. King
Bill Clinton
Bill Gates
Bob Dole
Bono
Cher
Elton John
Elvira
Eminem
Fergie
Gerald Ford
John Glenn
Kate Moss
Liberace
Mary Hart
Mia Hamm
Neil Young
P. Diddy
Pele
Prince
Rihanna
Seal
Selena
Shakira
Star Jones
Steffi Graf
Will Smith

```
A A J K A T E M O S S A H W C
N E I L Y O U N G J R E X Y H
S T A R J O N E S I C U A M E
N W B G O Q O E V V M L L L R
B I I E H M T L I B E R A C E
B L L R N A E A N N R I C E A
K L L A G F S H A K I R A N I
I S C L L B O B D O L E E J E
N M L D E J E B X D B L D L A
G I I F N F E R G I E O E N L
B T N O N B M H U S M P N D G
R H T R P R I N C E F A E O O
U L O D W T N M I A H A M M R
E C N T S T E F F I G R A F E
P D I D D Y M A R Y H A R T C
```

6		7			4			
1			2		8			
	5			1		6		
		5				4		
			4		2			3
						9	2	8
	2			4				
7			1		3			
4	8					1		

							9	2
4	8					3		
	9	5	7					
7	6		3	4			5	
1							6	
	3							
		8	2		9	6		
					3	9		
			6				8	4

A	T	E	P	E	T	O	R	K	B	E	I	G	H	F	T
B	L	E	R	I	T	E	S	A	E	L	N	O	T		
D	H	S	P	E	A	I	S	N	L	S	S	H	A		
T	O	E		D	I	S		E	E	I	T	G			
H	H	E							L						

Random Thoughts...

Do Vegetarians eat animal crackers?

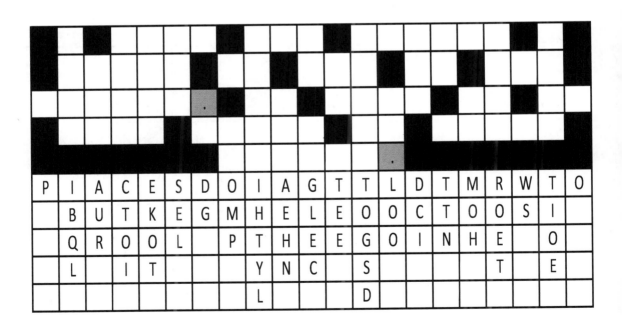

ARE YOU CHEAP ?

Being frugal is an admirable quality. But when it crosses the line into cheap...
not so good. Take this test to see if you're a penny pincher!

Have you ever re-gifted a present?	yes		no	
Do you regularly shop at the Dollar Tree?	yes		no	
Have you ever been lectured for not leaving a big enough tip?	yes		no	
Do you clip coupons every week?	yes		no	
Do you compare prices on almost everything you buy?	yes		no	
Do you prefer to calculate everyones dinner portion instead of dividing it equally?	yes		no	
Do you pick up every penny you see laying on the ground?	yes		no	
Do you always order off of the value menu?	yes		no	
Do you buy discounted meat or milk?	yes		no	
Do you only buy clothes if they're on sale?	yes		no	
Have you ever bought a brand new car?	no		yes	
Do other people think that you're poor?	yes		no	
Score 1 point for each answer in the first column TOTAL =				

WHAT DOES YOUR SCORE MEAN ?

0-4...If you're not lacking for money, keep doing what you're doing. You're definitely not cheap. If you find that you're short sometimes, you should try some money saving ideas.

5-8...You love hunting down a great deal, but you're also willing to spend your money. You have a good handle on your money.

9-12... You are so concerned about saving money that you are getting obsessed. Loosen up and enjoy life a little!

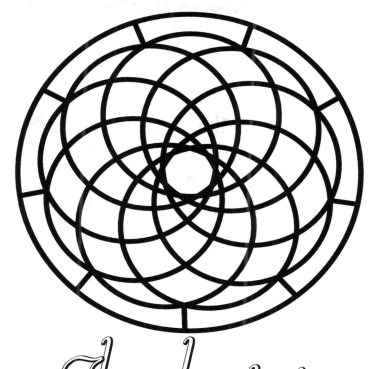

The best is

yet to come

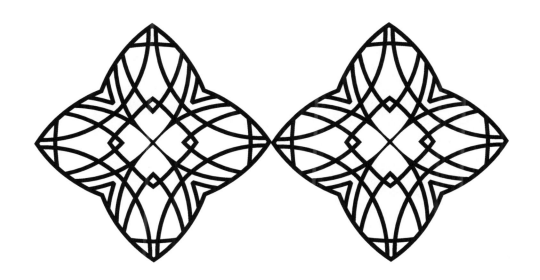

CROSSWORD 5

Across

1 Live wire, so to speak
3 Clod chopper
7 Restraining order?
9 I.R.S. employee: Abbr.
11 Mint family member
13 Hangup
14 Trips
16 Dirty coat
17 Motor suffix, commercially
18 This puzzle's theme (3,5,5)
21 "Fancy that!"
22 French pronoun
24 Nonsense
26 Kids Racer (2-4)
27 Barely get, with "out"
28 Trophy
29 End of the quip
31 Baker's dozen?
32 Picture starring 11D/55D (5,4,6)
33 Boat propellers
35 A.C. letters
37 Functions
39 ___-Mart
40 Even if, briefly
41 "Idylls of the King" character
43 Abbr. on a French envelope
44 They hold tin cups
45 1960's radical grp.
46 Keystone character

(numbers at the end of clues indicate multiple word answer and their letter count)

Down

2 Biochemistry abbr.
3 Birthright
4 "Chicago" lyricist
5 Central Park sight
6 Shabby
7 Colorful language (4-6,5)
8 "___ Perpetua" (Idaho's motto)
10 Coup ___
12 Brit. record label
15 Hon (7-3)
16 Direct
19 Turn in (3,3,3)
20 Rage (5,4)
23 Set off
25 Goes postal (5,2)
30 Fix, as a pump
34 Gonorrhea, e.g.: Abbr.
35 Hard knocks
36 Admiral's org.
37 Fat unit
38 Armageddon
40 French possessive
42 AOL, e.g.
43 French title abbr.

49

arrowroot
basket
Bath bun
beat
beer
besom
bread
can
carafe
chef
chianti
chuck
cloche
cob
crown
dish
eggs
escalope
flan
goose
gruyere
haunch of mutton
hot
ice box
match
mess
mixer
mug
mulled cider

pease
rare
reduce
roll
salad
shank
simnel
soup
soy
syrup
tea
tomato
trace
trap
trivet
tub
tuna
urn
vegetable cutter
waffle
yolk

```
T U N A I G R U Y E R E N N G A Q
E O G D S Z M H H U E F S V U R N
G N M Z K H W S C P D G Y E P R N
C H I A N T I E J L U B R G H O O
S O U P T D P E S X C E U E T W P
F N Z C Z O U G O X E E P T R R H
W A F F L E G B C Q P R U A I O O
C A R A F E E U A N E M C B V O T
N H C L O C H E N X F E O L E T Y
B S U R I A S L I O L S T E T O C
E E B C O S I M H L A S R C S M O
S H A N K W M C D P N E A U T U B
O S S T L P N A M Q S Y C T F G E
M A K N A U E Z T O J T E T N R Y
A L E R A R L A O C H E F E A K O
B A T H B U N G S H H A C R O L L
H D C R R M U L L E D C I D E R K
```

1	6			5				
	5	9			8			
				7				
			2		3			9
	2		7			5		8
	8				6		7	
	4				2		1	
						6	9	2
								7

2		6				4		
	8			9			1	
						7		
5			8		6		3	
7					9		4	
		2				1		
			6					3
				4			2	
			9	2	8	5		

T	A	R	E	S	M	E	D	I	F	I	A	R	W	N	T	O		A
M	I	K	E	Y	A	U	E	Q	U	F	E	K	L	Y	C	H		
	R	F		L	O	S	T	H	I	T	O	E	I	T	U			
	A	Y		T	O	O	P	I	M	N	L		O	E				
				O			S	N	G									

Random Thoughts...

A boiled egg is hard to beat.

Puzzle 14

D	R	T	N	E	O	E	R	W	E	H	H	E	S	M	E	H	T	I	N	N
B	I	S	W	H	R	O	U	T	T	T	S	E	B	E	E	T	O	W	I	
O	I	C	O	V	U	R	S	W	L	E	E	E	B	S	T	O				
		H	G	E	S		E	E	V	S	O	K		S						
			N																	

Puzzle 15

M	A	S	T	T	H	O	I	K	D	A	K	R	Y
T	O	E	U	T	F	A	S	N	M	A	P	E	P
A	B	S	I	R	O	M	L	E	H	S	A	P	E
	H	O		T		E	B		S			U	
						Y							

SUPER FOODS QUIZ

Super foods are foods that contribute above average health benefits. See if you can find the benefit that the Super Foods below are best know for.

Avocados _____

Sweet Potatoes _____

Walnuts _____

Kim Chi _____

Organic Eggs _____

Kale _____

Unsweetened Yogurt _____

Salmon _____

Turmeric _____

Coconut Oil _____

Chia Seeds _____

Blueberries _____

Green Tea _____

Olive Oil _____

Quinoa _____

A.   Great for your brain, memory and packed with healthy fat and fiber. Great in salads and cookies.

B.   A gluten free supergrain higher in protein and fiber than most other grains.

C.   Boosts the immune system and contains probiotics.

D.   Source of fat that increases good cholesterol. Might actually help with burning fat.

E.   Excellent source of antioxidants, boosts focus and memory and linked to helping prevent skin cancer. Also, they're really good in muffins.

F.   Full of healthy monounsaturated fats and linked to a healthy heart. Sensitive to light and high heat.

G.   Tiny whole grain that's full of omega-3 fatty acids, fiber, antioxidants and minerals. Can be used as a thickener.

H.   Contains probiotic that aids in digestion. Traditional Korean food.

I.   Orange color indicative of its excellent source of Vitamin A, beta-carotene and fiber.

J.   Super anti-cancer properties, especially against prostate cancer.

K.   Contains a high level of healthy Omega-3 fatty acids that reduces inflammation. Best if sourced from the wild instead of farmed.

L.   Packed with antioxidants and anti-inflammatory properties, this food is also nonfat and full of vitamins. Common in Indian cuisine.

M.   Contains healthy unsaturated fat and fiber and more potassium than bananas. They are technically a fruit and will ripen quicker with an apple nearby.

N.   Low in calories, high in fiber, zero fat, packed with Vitamin A, C and K and antioxidants. Bake and salt for a healthy replacement for chips.

O.   Full of protein, B-Vitamins, choline, lutein and often called the perfect food.

Avocados...M, Sweet Potatoes...I, Walnuts ...A, Kim Chi...H, Organic Eggs ...O, Kale...N, Unsweetened Yogurt...C, Salmon...K, Turmeric...L, Coconut Oil...D, Chia Seeds...G, Blueberries...E, Green Tea...J, Olive Oil...F, Quinoa...B.

Have faith in
your strength

59

CROSSWORD 6

Across

1 Feelers
4 Boeing 747, e.g.
6 "How's tricks?" (5,3)
10 Dry riverbed
12 Popular cocktail (7,4)
16 Cracker Jack bonus
17 Former Serbian capital
19 1814 Byron poem
20 High ground (3,8,4)
22 Quite some time (1,5,2,7)
24 Cheap
25 Shrink
26 The "p" in m.p.g.
27 Nonstop (3,2,3,3,3)
30 Angry
32 Kind of network
35 About (2,2)
37 Develop
40 Ecstasy
42 Italian for "to the tooth" (2,5)
44 Parade
45 Disoriented
49 Do followers
51 Carpentry tool
52 One of the Kennedys
53 Invoice abbr.
54 See circled squares

(numbers at the end of clues indicate multiple word answer and their letter count)

Down

1 Freely (2,4)
2 Rx instruction
3 Book after Galatians: Abbr.
4 Madison or Monroe: Abbr.
5 Athletic supporter?
6 Tony and Maria Musical (4,4,5)
7 Prefix with pressure
8 Unappealing (3,4,3,2,3)
9 Explanations
11 Because (2,2,4,2)
13 Better (7,2)
14 "Rock and Roll, Hoochie ___" (1974 hit)
15 Puts back on eBay
18 Loud
21 Kind of race
23 Reputation ruiner (10,5)
25 Engine sound
28 "Aladdin" monkey
29 Mrs. Addams, to Gomez
31 Dressed (up)
33 Brontë's "Jane ___"
34 Lift (4,3)
36 Expels
37 Veteran
38 "___ cost to you!" (2,2)
39 Nutty confection
41 Expunges
43 Chinese "way"
46 "The wolf ___ the door"
47 Math class, for short
48 ...
49 "In the Good Old Summertime" lyricist Shields
50 Medical suffix

WORD FIND 6 - JOBS

Accountant
Architect
Artist
Baker
Buyer
Care assistant
Caretaker
Carpenter
Cashier
Chef
Chemist
Civil servant
Cleaner
Clerk
Cook
Counsellor
Courier
Doctor
Driver
Editor
Engineer
Farmer
IT manager
Lawyer

Lecturer
Librarian
Mechanic
Musician
Nanny
Nurse
Physicist
Pilot
Plumber
Printer
Production manager
Surgeon
Teacher
Trainer
Turner
Tutor
Typist
Waiter
Waitress
Welder

```
W A I T R E S S G V F R R U T T F H C
A L A W Y E R E K A T E R A C N E D A
I R T S I T R A R R Y I S C E A H X E
T C N E C N D M A U Z R U C T V C P X
E N I Z F O E I B B E U R O I R S R R
R C N N C R N P R K Q O G U H E R E E
I H T T A E F E A V N C E N C S E T R
U C O N R H V B Z P I A O T R L T N U
I R L M A I C W Z C E L N A A I N E T
T H I E R T R E N A E L C N J V I P C
M P B D R T S I M E H C B T Y I R R E
A W R A X K O I T R E I H S A C P A L
N N A M A D R F S Y T E A C H E R C L
A U R E D L E W G S P H Y S I C I S T
G R I P H K N X Y N A I C I S U M R P
E S A U Y O R R O L L E S N U O C O I
R E N S E O U E D I T O R T V N E T L
P R O D U C T I O N M A N A G E R U O
E N G I N E E R E B M U L P C H W T T
```

		5			1	4	3	
					9			8
		7	2				1	
			3	9				2
		9				8		
1				5	7			
	6				8	2		
5			1					
	7	8	6			3		

SUDOKU 12 - MEDIUM

7	9							2
6			7		2			9
	3							
					8		2	1
					6	3		
			9	1			8	7
		1	8		4			
			3					
		5					9	8

F	R	L	L	U	R	S	G	I	Y	O	U	O	T	N	G
S	U	O	C	T	S	E	S	L	A	T	E	R	U	O	
F	A	E	M	S	I	U	I	W	I	S	G	O	I	T	
	I	N	E	H	A		I		U	R	H				
		C	O		F	N				S		M			

Dumb Joke...

What's the difference between snowmen and snowwomen?

(answer on page 110)

FALLEN QUOTES – 17, 18

Puzzle 17

					,						.	
F	A	F	L	N	O	Y	O	D	Y	O	R	E
F	T	C	E	L	W	A	O	Y	I	U	R	
S	A	V	E	R		M	F	V	O	N	G	
	E	I	L			I	R	U		A	U	
		L	O			N						

Puzzle 18

							,						.			
I	G	R	A	S	E	N	U	L	A	K	H	U	P	P	S	A	S	S
T	R	T	T	E	T	O	M	S	E	S	P	T	T	Y	E	E
G	M	A	K	E	F	U	T	N	H	B	S	P	U	H	H	T
	A	H	A	F		U			A	A			I	N		
	I	T		S		L			E	S			T			

NATURAL REMEDIES

Below are some surprisingly effective and inexpensive home remedies. See if you can match them with what they are proven to help treat.
(this test is just for fun - please check with your doctor before trying to use anything to treat your symptoms)!

Ginger _____

Linden Flower Tea _____

Oatmeal _____

Tea with lemon and honey _____

Two teaspoons of sugar _____

Cherries _____

Aloe Vera _____

Gargling with garlic and warm water _____

Two squares dark chocolate or honey _____

Peppermint tea _____

A.   Can reduce the length of a cold

B.   Curbs a cough

C.   Sooths a burn

D.   Quells nausea

E.   Stops hiccups

F.   Soothes sore throats and wards off vampires

G.   Helps you sleep

H.   Reduces fever

I.   Prevents farting...or at least makes them smell a little better

J.   Steeped in water will help relieve dry itchy skin

Ginger...D, Linden Flower Tea...H, Oatmeal ..J, Tea with lemon and honey...B, Two teaspoons
of sugar ...E, Cherries...G, Aloe Vera...C, Garling with garlic and warm water...F,
Two squares of dark chocolate or honey...A, Peppermint Tea...L
Blueberries...E, Green Tea...J, Olive Oil...F, Quinoa...B.

Live life in color

CROSSWORD 7

Across

1 Garden decorations
4 Mercedes competitor
6 Bluecoat
9 Butt
11 Retreats
14 Red state
16 Part of E.E.C.: Abbr.
18 "Beats me" (1,6,3,1,4)
21 Long Island town
22 Danger signal
23 Sailing ropes
24 P.I., e.g.
25 Trunk item (3,6)
27 Surrounding glows
28 ___ cry
29 Proportionately (3,4)
30 The "S" in R.S.V.P.
31 A abroad
32 Ancient
33 Destroy
34 Awakens (5,2)
36 Head honcho (3,9)
38 Full of vigor
40 ___-Locka, Fla.
41 Combination punch?
43 Airs
45 Acrylic fiber
46 Fuddy-duddy (3-9)

Down

2 Masefield play "The Tragedy of ___"
3 Yemen, once
5 Heads overseas?
6 Creamy desserts with ladyfingers (9,6)
7 "Easy!" (5,2,4)
8 California's ___ Valley
10 Crumble (2,2,6)
12 Hard to grasp (8,2,2,3)
13 Suffix with sermon (0-3)
15 Boris Godunov, for one
17 Fast (9,6)
19 Kilmer of "At First Sight"
20 This puzzle's theme (3,5,5)
22 "Wow!"
26 Danish cheese
28 Fast one
29 Brownish purple
34 Pandemonium
35 Jazz trombonist Kid ___
37 Comedians real name was Arthur
39 Bit of color
41 Scooby-___ (cartoon dog)
42 Gonorrhea, e.g.: Abbr.
44 Altar avowal

(numbers at the end of clues indicate multiple word answer and their letter count)

72

WORD FIND 7 - MUSICAL INSTRUMENTS

accordion
anvil
banjo
bellharp
bin
bones
bugelhorn
bugle
cello
cheng
chimes
citar
clarinet
crwth
cymbal
ditalharp
dulcimer
electronic piano
fife
flute
gong
guitar
hand bell
hurdygurdy
klavier
lyre
mandolin
marina
melotron
moog
oboe

organ
pipe
quail
rattle
rebec
shawm
snare drum
stock horn
tabor
tambour
timpani
tromba
tuba
vina
viola
violin
virginal
zimbalon
zither

```
Q P X E R K V F C N E C C T B O N E S
T T O Z L R W R I H L I G U I T A R K
I R B I K X E B Q M E A N V I L A H M
M O O M G I Z N H W C N O T K T M X N
P M E B V Z I I U A T Z G Z I N Z I W
A B A A A U T L R H R A V C Q R L Y R
N A L L S T H O D S O N M B B O V V U
I K S O O O E I Y L N I A A D H D R O
D V R N S I R V G C I R R N N K U E B
P I A B U T V B U L C A A J O C S M M
C R T T N Z U D R A P M U O I O N I A
R G T A C G R E D R I Z E Q D T A C T
W I L Q L Y R E Y I A W C L R S R L F
T N E E E H M K B N N N H E O M E U I
H A B V O P A B P E O A I Y C T D D F
R L R L K X I R A T C G M V C E R L E
B E L L H A R P P L Q R E O A X U O M
T E L L E B D N A H J O S M O T M T N
C I P I A Z M H K N R O H L E G U B D
```

9		7			5			
	8	2			3	4	7	
					8			2
	3		6	9			8	
4			8			2		
	2							
			5			9		
1	5			7			6	
		4						

				3	8			6
4							3	
			4	2			9	
	5	8						
	4			9				1
		1			3			5
		6						7
	2						6	
	9		6			1	8	

W	O	I	W	H	E	E	G	N	L	B	S	Y	A	O	T	H	T	N	S	S
W	A	O	P	Y	I	N	O	S	A	I	U	W	T	N	I	T	I	H	G	E
H	H	P	C	E	R	A	S	F		B	E	R	O	W	D	C	O	A	E
	P	R	T	I	N		O	E		Y	O	U	T	Y		L	E	
		R	H			R		O							L	

Dumb Joke...

What do you call a bear with no teeth?

(answer on page 110)

FALLEN QUOTES - 20, 21

Today can be
filled with joy

CROSSWORD 8

Across

1 Chicken
3 Abase
6 French pronoun
9 Drawing
13 Dirty coat
14 Living
17 Ascap alternative
18 Neighbor of Tenn.
20 Repeating
21 Stink
22 Hearst's captors: Abbr.
24 Blouse, e.g.
26 Some are vital
27 Curt
29 "Lord, is ___?"
30 Big inits. in trucks
31 Head, slangily
32 Scale notes
33 Loc. ___
34 Milk: Prefix
36 City on the Susquehanna
37 Bird ___
38 "___ Doone" (1869 novel)
40 Cooler
41 Nonconformists
42 "La la" preceder
43 Boom producer
47 Inner: Prefix
48 Desire (5,3)
49 "How ___ Has the Banshee Cried"
(Thomas Moore poem) (7,8)

*(numbers at the end of clues indicate
multiple word answer and their letter
count)*

Down

1 China's Sun ___-sen
2 K-O connection
4 not your
5 Jimmy Stewart syllables
6 Tops (3,4)
7 Direct (2,3,5)
8 Part of BYO
10 Here, elsewhere
11 Quits (5,2,3,5)
12 Goodwill, e.g. (10,5)
15 "Rocky ___"
16 International understanding (7,8)
17 flock with each other (5,2,1,7)
19 Sue Grafton's "___ for Alibi"
23 "___ Olvidados" (1950 Luis
Buñuel film)
25 Relish
28 Carefree
30 Magnanimousness
35 Join, redundantly (5,2)
39 QB protectors
44 L.B.J.'s successor
45 Tokyo, formerly
46 Buffalo's summer hrs.

Adam	laver
Anglican	limbo
Calvinistical	Lot
cardinal	Magi
clean	manna
cosher	minor
damned	missal
Daniel	mortal
deadly	nonkosher
dean	nuncio
doomed	parable
errancy	pax
Esau	Rota
Esther	Russian Orthodox
Eve	Seder
gradual	shibah
Hallel	shiva
Haman	Sodom
Hell	tref
impure	venial
Inferno	
Jacob	
Jonah	
Joseph	
Last Day	

```
Y D C N E I G A M Z X X E Y E J D
N A J W A L R B P A X O L S O T P
I M D L L E A E C A R D I N A L S
M N E T H I D R D E A O A O N U H
P E M S S N U R V E V H X N G B I
U D O L X A A A D T S T D K L O B
R C O I A D L N G O L R G O I C A
E R D M M T P C M L A O X S C A H
C V A B C O O Y I E I N H H A J F
M D J O I W R R S E N A P E N E E
A I C I N J H T S F E I E R R N L
N O N L F W H A A Q V S S T D A B
N S H O E E U V L L C S O D O M A
A N J P R A O S Q L G U J C R A R
E D G W N U N C I O E R W I R H A
V V V X O L S H I V A L H E L L P
F O E D L A C I T S I N I V L A C
```

			3		7			
		9	4				8	
			8		1	9		
		3	2			1		
		2				3		
	8		1		3	7		
	3		5	4				
6		4		1				
	7				8			6

				4	7	2		
7			2		9			
	9				3	1	4	
		9						
			5				8	
	1	3		7				
		5				3		8
1								
	7		1	2				9

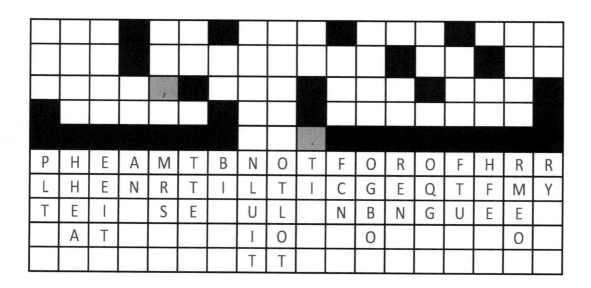

P	H	E	A	M	T	B	N	O	T	F	O	R	O	F	H	R	R
L	H	E	N	R	T	I	L	T	I	C	G	E	Q	T	F	M	Y
T	E	I		S	E		U	L		N	B	N	G	U	E	E	
	A	T					I	O				O				O	
							T	T									

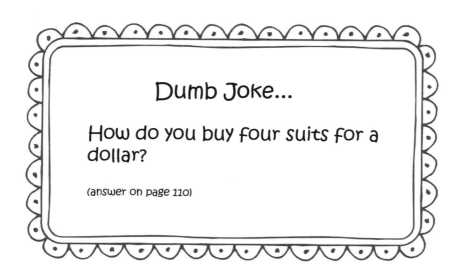

Dumb Joke...

How do you buy four suits for a dollar?

(answer on page 110)

You deserue happiness

CROSSWORD 9

Across

1 Not coming after down (9,2)
6 Dash
8 Colorful language (4-6,5)
11 "Be quiet!"
12 Unified
13 Dadaism founder
15 Allergic reaction
17 Big ___ Conference
18 Certain Scandinavian
20 Embraces
21 Blah-blah-blah
22 Boob tubes
23 Devours (8,3)
28 Binge
30 Sonora shawls
32 Help for checkers
33 Chiang ___-shek
34 Dude
36 BBQ annoyance
38 Chip off the old block
40 1956 Elvis song (10,5)

*(numbers at the end of clues in-
dicate multiple word answer and
their letter count)*

Down

1 Marching band instruments
2 End of the query
3 Jerk
4 Score
5 Revolts
6 Detachable container
7 3.1415
9 Render unnecessary
10 Green light (5,2,8)
14 El ___, Tex.
16 Hack
17 Puts two and two together?
(5,2)
19 Suffix with president
24 Small carriage (3-6)
25 Bits
26 Lodge
27 Pool opening
29 Clear
31 Atl. crosser
35 "Stupid me!"
36 Little, in Leith
37 Biochemistry abbr.
39 "Flying Down to ___"

WORD FIND 9 - BRANDS

Band Aid
bennie
Carboloy
Clorox
Colt
Duralumin
Gortex
Hoover
Invar
Kleenex
Lilo
Loafer
Lucite
Luger
Maalox
Magic Marker
Masonite
Meccano
Mylanta
Orlon
Xerox

Perspex
Pyrex
Rolaids
Scotch tape
Scrabble
Silex
Sno-cat
Spam
Stellite
Styrofoam
Teflon
Thermos
Tums
Velcro
Viyella
Xerox

```
M V L U C I T E T H E R M O S E L
A A U O L I L O D P T X V C I X J
T U G A B E N N I E I T L O C R W
N P E I S N O C A T L T X O R E X
A S R K C V W X D I L C O M R F B
L S T L R M B C N T E F L O N A P
Y C K E A H A D A I T H A O J O Y
M O E E B W D R B Q S W A E R L R
S T E N B U Z U K E X N M Z M O E
P C V E L C R O R E P E R S P E X
A H H X E E F V G A R O L A I D S
M T G O R T E X V V L N U I T V K
C A R B O L O Y E E A U O U S E N
A P A H Z V Q I N V A R M L D W C
Y E M V I Y E L L A L S S I R I C
M E C C A N O R D V U K Z P N O X
M A S O N I T E M A O F O R Y T S
```

					6			2
					4			
			5	9	2	4		1
7	3						6	
6			2	1		5		
		9						
	8				1			3
				8			4	6
2			7					8

6						5		
						6		3
7		9		8	6			
	1				8		4	
			7					
			2	6			8	1
		6	9					
	7						2	
4		2				9		

Dumb Joke...

How do fish get high?

(answer on page 110)

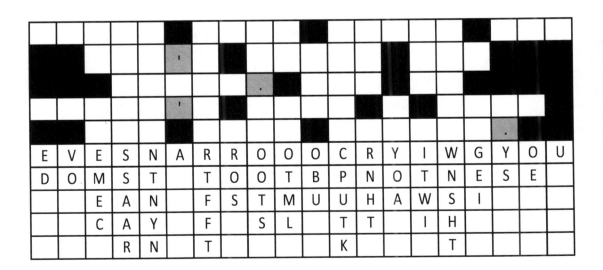

USA HISTORY TRIVIA QUESTIONS

How well do you know USA History? Take the quiz below to find out!

1. Who said "Give me liberty or give me death?" _____

2. What year did the Civil War Start? _____

3. Who said, "I regret that I have only one life to give for my country?" _____

4. Who was the second president of the United States? _____

5. The Battle of the Bulge occurred during what War? _____

6. How many amendments to the Constitution are there? _____

7. How many branches of the US Government are there? _____

8. Who was the first U.S. president to appear on television? _____

9. What year did Congress pass the right of woman to vote? _____

10. True or False? American currency is backed by gold. _____

11. Machine guns were first used during which World War? _____

12. What is the only amendment to be repealed? _____

13. Who is the only president that served more than 2 terms? _____

14. How many presidents have been assassinated while in office? _____

15. What year was Wall Street Crash, also known as Black Tuesday? _____

a.   Franklin Delano Roosevelt

b.   1

c.   Patrick Henry

d.   1919

e.   4

f.   Franklin Roosevelt

g.   Nathan Hale

h.   2

i.   27

j.   3

k.   1861

l.   false

m.   18

n.   1929

o.   John Adams

1...c, 2...k, 3...g, 4...o, 5...h, 6...i, 7...j, 8...f, 9...d, 10...l, 11...b, 12...m, 13...a, 14...e, 15...n

CROSSWORD 10

Across

2 No-show
6 Had a tiger for a shipmate
7 Hair salon stock
9 Office stations
10 Ltr. holder
12 Circus Hall of Fame site
14 "Absolutely!"
17 Do, re, mi
18 Relief
19 Carpentry tool
20 Animation
22 Somehow (3,3,2,7)
27 Lousy
28 Witch
29 Fib
31 Extol
33 Outhouse? (4,3,3,5)
34 Poets' feet
35 Vital engine conduit (3,4)
36 Improvise (4,2)
37 Sitting room?
38 They're full of beans

Down

1 Special delivery?
2 Mar, in a way
3 But, to Brutus
4 Quit
5 Failing grades
6 Ballpoint, e.g.
7 Pay (up)
8 Tiara wearer (4,7)
10 Book after Proverbs: Abbr.
11 Swerve
13 Duct opening?
15 Buffalo's AAA baseball team
16 Send to the canvas
20 Battery units
21 Quip, part 2
22 Fuddy-duddy (3-9)
23 Not permanent
24 How this answer is situated (5,2,4)
25 Spring event (5,6)
26 Beat
29 Big brass
30 Heartfelt
32 Rattle

(numbers at the end of clues indicate multiple word answer and their letter count)

102

WORD FIND 10 - VEGETABLES

bean

beet

broccoli

caper

capsicum

carrot

celeriac

celery

chard

chicory

chili

chive

cole

corn

cos lettuce

courgette

cress

endive

eschalot

fitch

giant shallot

gourd

kale

King Edward

leek

lentil

maize

nettle

okra

onion

parsnip

pea

plantain

potato

pulse

radish

red pepper

sage

soy

swede

tomato

turnip

yam

```
E W X F Y T C O D P L A N T A I N
T C Y R S M O R A D I S H U V Z M
D O A R F A L L P U L S E C T X L
R O R P E Y E C A O E S E A O T E
A T C R S L H K H H T T L P L X E
H A C E A I E Y I I C A T E L A K
C M X R L C C C M N V S T R A S D
E O H I E E M U O O G E E O H C R
D T S C S S R C M I T E N P S H E
I R T L T W S I U N R N D M T I P
L F O E E I E H A O I D A W N C P
I B Z S G T F D Y C A I Y T A O E
T D A H B R T R E R Z V B E I R P
N G B Y E R U U K E C E S E G Y D
E Q J O A B R O C C O L I B Z H E
L K O S N E M G C E T U R N I P R
P I N S R A P Z A W P C O R N B K
```

SUDOKU 20 - HARD

	6		2			5		3
						9		1
3		5	9					
	9			6		4	8	
		2			4			5
5				7				
4								
	8				7	2	4	9

U	H	T	I	O	D	T	O	R	O	F	T	O	F	O
W	T	E	T	L	R	O	P	U	A	A	N	E	W	
N	H	V	E	Y	O	R	M	C	W	O	F	R		
N	A	T		M		A	U		T	R	R		D	
		E				Y			O					

Dumb Joke...

What is the dumbest animal in the jungle?

(answer on page 110)

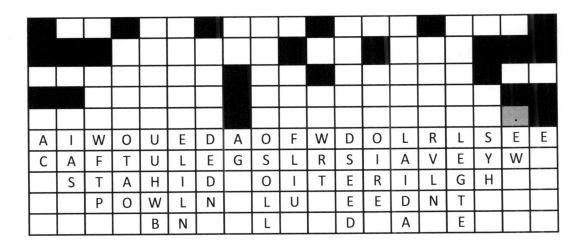

FIND SOMEONE WHO....

Communicating with other people is proven to improve overall health. See if you can find someone who... Score a point for every one you find!

_____ owns more than three pets.

_____ takes baths instead of showers.

_____ has visited more than 5 countries.

_____ has made beer.

_____ speaks more than 2 languages.

_____ does not like broccoli.

_____ who has been in a play.

_____ has had their tonsils removed.

_____ sings in a choir.

_____ who has more than 5 siblings.

May the road rise up to meet you.
May the wind be always at your back.
May the sun shine warm upon your face.
And rains fall soft upon your fields.
And until we meet again,
May God hold you in the hollow of His hand.

Irish Blessing

Crossword 1 - page 3

Crossword 2 - page 15

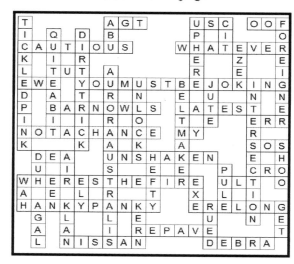

Crossword 3 - page 27

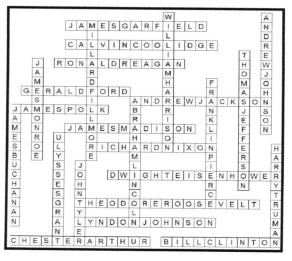

Crossword 4 - page 37

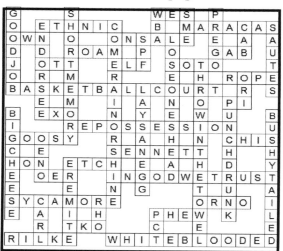

Crossword 5 - page 49

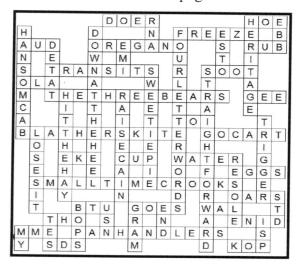

Crossword 6 - page 61

Crossword 7 - page 73

Crossword 8 - page 83

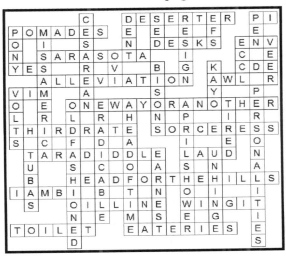

Crossword 9 - page 93

Crossword 10 - page 103

Word Find 1 - page 5

Word Find 2 - page 17

Word Find 3 - page 29

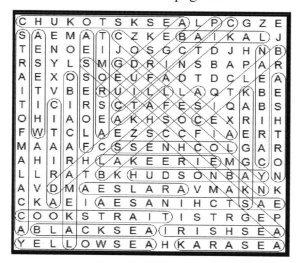

Word Find 4 - page 39

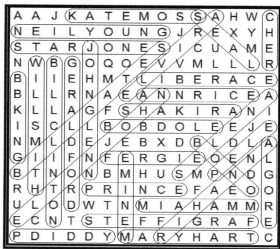

Word Find 5 - page 51

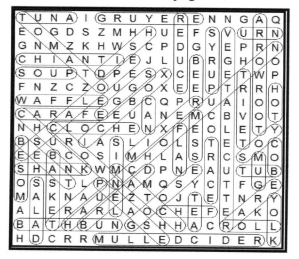

Word Find 6 - page 63

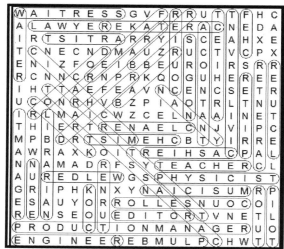

Word Find 7 - page 75

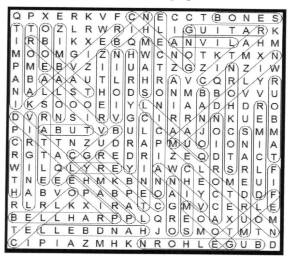

Word Find 8 - page 85

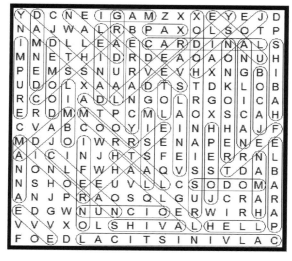

Word Find 9 - page 95

```
M V L U C I T E T H E R M O S E L
A U A U O L I L O D P T X V C I X J
T U G A B E N N I E I T L O C R W
N P E I S N O C A T L T X O R E X
A S R K C V W X D I L C O M R F B
L Y S T L R M B C N T E F L O N A P
M O K E E A H A D A I T H A O J O Y
S P T C E E B W D R B Q S W A E R L R
P A H V E L C R O R E P E R S P E X
A M T H X E E F V G A R O L A I D S
C A R B O L O Y E E A U O U S E N
A P A H Z V Q I N V A R M L D W C
Y E M V I Y E L L A L S S R I C
M E C C A N O R D V U K Z P N O X
M A S O N I T E M A O F O R Y T S
```

Word Find 10 - page 105

```
E W X F Y T C O D P L A N T A I N
T C Y R S M O R A D I S H U V Z M
D O A R F A L L P U L S E C T X L
R O R P E Y E C A O E S E A O T E
A T C R S L H K H H T T L P L X E
H A C E A I E Y I I C A T E L A K
C M X R L C C C M N V S T R A S D
E O H I E E M U O O G E C H O H C
D T S C S S R C M I T E N P S H I
I R T L T W S I U N R N D M T N O
L F O E E I E H A O I D A W N C R
I B Z S G T E D Y C A I T A O Y
T D A H B R T R E R Z V B E I R
N G B Y E R U U K E C E S E G Y D
E Q J O A B R O C C O L I B Z H E
L K O S N E M G C E T U R N I P R
P I N S R A P Z A W P C O R N B K
```

Sudoku 1 - page 6

3	6	9	7	2	8	1	4	5
7	2	1	4	9	5	3	6	8
8	4	5	1	6	3	9	7	2
1	5	2	6	7	9	4	8	3
6	9	3	8	5	4	7	2	1
4	7	8	2	3	1	5	9	6
9	1	4	3	8	2	6	5	7
5	8	6	9	1	7	2	3	4
2	3	7	5	4	6	8	1	9

Sudoku 2 - page 7

7	4	8	3	2	6	9	1	5
3	9	5	8	4	1	2	6	7
6	1	2	7	5	9	3	4	8
9	5	7	2	1	4	6	8	3
4	8	1	6	3	7	5	2	9
2	6	3	5	9	8	4	7	1
1	7	4	9	6	5	8	3	2
5	3	6	1	8	2	7	9	4
8	2	9	4	7	3	1	5	6

Sudoku 3 - page 18

8	9	5	7	3	4	1	6	2
6	3	4	9	1	2	8	7	5
1	7	2	5	8	6	4	9	3
3	5	7	8	9	1	2	4	6
2	6	1	3	4	7	5	8	9
9	4	8	2	6	5	3	1	7
4	1	3	6	2	9	7	5	8
5	8	9	1	7	3	6	2	4
7	2	6	4	5	8	9	3	1

Sudoku 4 - page 19

3	5	1	6	7	9	4	2	8
9	8	2	1	5	4	6	3	7
6	7	4	2	8	3	9	1	5
2	4	5	3	9	8	7	6	1
7	9	6	5	1	2	3	8	4
8	1	3	7	4	6	5	9	2
5	2	7	9	6	1	8	4	3
4	3	9	8	2	5	1	7	6
1	6	8	4	3	7	2	5	9

Sudoku 5 - page 30

6	8	4	9	1	2	5	7	3
2	3	9	6	5	7	1	4	8
5	7	1	8	3	4	9	6	2
1	6	3	5	4	8	2	9	7
8	5	7	3	2	9	4	1	6
4	9	2	7	6	1	8	3	5
7	1	6	4	8	5	3	2	9
3	2	8	1	9	6	7	5	4
9	4	5	2	7	3	6	8	1

Sudoku 6 - page 31

3	7	4	8	9	2	5	1	6
8	5	2	4	1	6	9	3	7
6	9	1	7	3	5	8	2	4
2	1	9	6	4	3	7	8	5
7	3	5	9	2	8	6	4	1
4	8	6	5	7	1	2	9	3
9	2	7	3	5	4	1	6	8
1	4	8	2	6	7	3	5	9
5	6	3	1	8	9	4	7	2

Sudoku 7 - page 40

6	3	7	5	9	4	8	1	2
1	4	9	2	6	8	7	3	5
8	5	2	3	1	7	6	4	9
2	6	5	8	3	9	4	7	1
9	1	8	4	7	2	5	6	3
3	7	4	6	5	1	9	2	8
5	2	1	9	4	6	3	8	7
7	9	6	1	8	3	2	5	4
4	8	3	7	2	5	1	9	6

Sudoku 8 - page 41

3	7	6	8	1	4	5	9	2
4	8	1	5	9	2	3	7	6
2	9	5	7	3	6	4	1	8
7	6	2	3	4	8	1	5	9
1	5	4	9	2	7	8	6	3
8	3	9	1	6	5	2	4	7
5	4	8	2	7	9	6	3	1
6	1	7	4	8	3	9	2	5
9	2	3	6	5	1	7	8	4

Sudoku 9 - page 52

1	6	7	3	5	9	8	2	4
4	5	9	6	2	8	7	3	1
8	3	2	4	7	1	9	5	6
6	7	5	2	8	3	1	4	9
3	2	1	7	9	4	5	6	8
9	8	4	5	1	6	2	7	3
7	4	8	9	6	2	3	1	5
5	1	3	8	4	7	6	9	2
2	9	6	1	3	5	4	8	7

Sudoku 10 - page 53

2	3	6	1	8	7	4	5	9
4	8	7	5	9	2	3	1	6
9	5	1	3	6	4	7	8	2
5	4	9	8	1	6	2	3	7
7	1	8	2	3	9	6	4	5
3	6	2	4	7	5	1	9	8
8	2	4	6	5	1	9	7	3
6	9	5	7	4	3	8	2	1
1	7	3	9	2	8	5	6	4

Sudoku 11 - page 64

2	8	5	7	6	1	4	3	9
6	1	3	5	4	9	7	2	8
9	4	7	2	8	3	5	1	6
8	5	4	3	9	6	1	7	2
7	3	9	4	1	2	8	6	5
1	2	6	8	5	7	9	4	3
3	6	1	9	7	8	2	5	4
5	9	2	1	3	4	6	8	7
4	7	8	6	2	5	3	9	1

Sudoku 12 - page 65

7	9	8	1	6	3	4	5	2
6	5	4	7	8	2	1	3	9
1	3	2	4	5	9	8	7	6
5	6	7	3	4	8	9	2	1
8	1	9	2	7	6	3	4	5
4	2	3	9	1	5	6	8	7
2	7	1	8	9	4	5	6	3
9	8	6	5	3	7	2	1	4
3	4	5	6	2	1	7	9	8

Sudoku 13 - page 76

9	1	7	4	2	5	8	3	6
6	8	2	9	1	3	4	7	5
3	4	5	7	6	8	1	9	2
5	3	1	6	9	2	7	8	4
4	9	6	8	5	7	2	1	3
7	2	8	3	4	1	6	5	9
2	7	3	5	8	6	9	4	1
1	5	9	2	7	4	3	6	8
8	6	4	1	3	9	5	2	7

Sudoku 14 - page 77

2	7	9	5	3	8	4	1	6
4	8	5	1	6	9	7	3	2
6	1	3	4	2	7	5	9	8
7	5	8	2	1	6	3	4	9
3	4	2	8	9	5	6	7	1
9	6	1	7	4	3	8	2	5
1	3	6	9	8	4	2	5	7
8	2	7	3	5	1	9	6	4
5	9	4	6	7	2	1	8	3

Sudoku 15 - page 86

4	6	8	3	9	7	5	2	1
3	1	9	4	2	5	6	8	7
5	2	7	8	6	1	9	3	4
7	4	3	2	8	9	1	6	5
1	5	2	6	7	4	3	9	8
9	8	6	1	5	3	7	4	2
8	3	1	5	4	6	2	7	9
6	9	4	7	1	2	8	5	3
2	7	5	9	3	8	4	1	6

Sudoku 16 - page 87

5	8	1	6	4	7	2	9	3
7	3	4	2	1	9	8	6	5
6	9	2	8	5	3	1	4	7
2	5	9	4	8	1	7	3	6
4	6	7	5	3	2	9	8	1
8	1	3	9	7	6	5	2	4
9	2	5	7	6	4	3	1	8
1	4	8	3	9	5	6	7	2
3	7	6	1	2	8	4	5	9

Sudoku 17 - page 96

4	9	5	1	7	6	3	8	2
1	2	7	8	3	4	6	9	5
8	6	3	5	9	2	4	7	1
7	3	2	4	5	8	1	6	9
6	4	8	2	1	9	5	3	7
5	1	9	3	6	7	8	2	4
9	8	4	6	2	1	7	5	3
3	7	1	9	8	5	2	4	6
2	5	6	7	4	3	9	1	8

Sudoku 18 - page 97

6	4	3	7	2	1	5	9	8
1	2	8	4	5	9	6	7	3
7	5	9	3	8	6	4	1	2
2	1	7	5	9	8	3	4	6
8	6	4	1	7	3	2	5	9
3	9	5	2	6	4	7	8	1
5	8	6	9	4	2	1	3	7
9	7	1	6	3	5	8	2	4
4	3	2	8	1	7	9	6	5

Sudoku 19 - page 106

5	6	1	8	4	2	9	3	7
8	9	4	1	3	7	5	2	6
2	3	7	9	6	5	4	8	1
3	4	9	7	1	8	6	5	2
7	5	2	6	9	4	3	1	8
6	1	8	5	2	3	7	4	9
1	8	5	3	7	6	2	9	4
9	2	6	4	5	1	8	7	3
4	7	3	2	8	9	1	6	5

Sudoku 20 - page 107

9	6	1	2	4	8	5	7	3
8	2	4	7	5	3	9	6	1
3	7	5	9	1	6	8	2	4
7	9	3	1	6	5	4	8	2
6	1	2	8	9	4	7	3	5
5	4	8	3	7	2	1	9	6
2	3	9	4	8	1	6	5	7
4	5	7	6	2	9	3	1	8
1	8	6	5	3	7	2	4	9

Quote Falls 1,2,3 - page 8, 9

1 - People say nothing is impossible, but I do nothing every day.

2 - Life is ten percent what happens to you and ninety percent how you react to it.

3 - It is during our darkest moments that we must focus to see the light.

Quote Falls 4,5,6 - page 20, 21

4 - I always wanted to be somebody, but now I realize I should have been more specific.

5 - If you are going through hell...keep going.

6 - If at first you don't succeed, you should not try skydiving.

Quote Falls 7,8,9 - page 32, 33

7 - If you are lonely dim the lights and put on a horror movie. Soon it won't feel like you are alone anymore.

8 - I would rather attempt to do something great and fail than to attempt nothing and succeed.

9 - Time flies like an arrow. Fruit flies like a banana.

Quote Falls 10, 11, 12 - page 42, 43

10 - Hope is being able to see that there is light despite all of the darkness.

11 - I wish everything in life was as easy as getting fat.

12 - I told the doctor I broke my leg in two places. He told me to quit going to those places.

Quote Falls 13, 14, 15 - page 54, 55

13 - If you think you are too small to make a difference, try sleeping with a mosquito.

14 - When we seek to discover the best in others, we somehow bring out the best in ourselves.

15 - Most folks are about as happy as they make their minds up to be.

Quote Falls 16, 17, 18- page 66, 67

16 - Success is going from failure to failure without losing your enthusiasm.

17 - Even if you fall on your face, you are still moving forward

18 - It is not happiness that makes us grateful, but the gratefulness that makes us happy.

Quote Falls 19, 20, 21 - page 78, 79

19 - The only way to happiness is to cease worrying about things which are beyond the power of our will.

20 - The great essentials for happiness in this life are something to do, something to love and something to hope for.

21 - No one has ever become poor by giving.

Quote Falls 22, 23, 24- page 88, 89

22 - Let me not beg for the stilling of my pain, but for the heart to conquer it.

23 - All the art of living lies in a fine mingling of letting go and holding on.

24 - You can move through life seeing nothing as a miracle, or seeing everything as a miracle.

25 - It isn't the mountains ahead to climb that wear you out; it's the pebble in your shoe.

26 - Smooth seas do not make skillful sailors.

27 - Every fool knows you can't touch the stars, but it doesn't stop a wise man from trying.

28 - Never put off until tomorrow what you can do the day after tomorrow.

29 - If you can't do great things, do small things in a great way.

30 - If we all did the things we are capable of doing we would literally astound ourselves.

Joke Answers

page 66 - snowballs

page 78 - gummi bears

page 88 - buy a deck of cards

page 98 - seaweed

page 108 - the polar bear